in the stranger's house

kelli fox

Copyright © 2021 by Kelli Fox

All rights reserved. No part of this book may be reproduced or used in any manner without written permission of the copyright owner except for the use of quotations in a book review.

First paperback edition December 2021

Photos by Kelli Fox

ISBN: 978-0-9998501-2-1 (paperback)
ISBN: 978-0-9998501-3-8 (ebook)

www.kelli-fox.work

"The river was rushing, and since it had no knowledge of anything beyond its own reality, it simply did its thing."

- Werner Herzog

the days slip past my outstretched fingertips,
bleeding into weeks,
        into months.
all of a sudden it's october
and my life has again adopted that
slightly frantic feeling of always running;
running hard and fast,
gasping
gulping in the air as it tears into my lungs,
a manic gleam to my eye as i grin
and then laugh
and then cannot stop laughing,
collapsing to the ground
clutching at the stitches in my side.

i am no longer a broken thing,
grasping at whatever reaches toward me,
packing trash instead of gauze
into the gaping wound,
watching as who i am bleeds swiftly from me.

cries rise from the streets
in collective joyous solidarity
humans behaving as animals,
               as coyotes,
               as wolves;
howling together to signify
something far larger than ourselves.

the landscape is rugged and wild and untamed,
rough and unforgiving in a way i wish to be.
only if one can bear its sharp, unrelenting edges
can one be truly rewarded with its beauty.
but sprawled at the base of the devil's throne
we comprehend our insignificant place
in the echelons of worlds
and epochs of time.

the sky will not hold fire tonight
but rather fade gently
from rose-tinged edgeless wisps
into a clear lilac twilight
without a moment's pause

eyes rain daylight
over freckled floodplains
we seal false envelopes
and abandon ourselves
            to the ether of early morning.

be with me, be with me
i'll take it in whatever way you'll give
the drippings off a roast are sometimes
the most delicious
give me, give me anything
i'll take it and spin it into gold
                       into love
                       into delusion
love me, love me *please*
i beg of you,
    of anyone
i am sad for all the seeds
that never got the chance to come to fruition
but desperation lies bitter in the nose
and lands heavy on the tongue

delusions i-iv

i.

he hands me a capri sun
and looks upon me in a mournful, piteous way
as he gently brushes a stray lock of hair
from my cheek.
i remember his hands the most clearly of all:
long, delicate piano player hands,
and the childish way he would look at me
that sometimes broke my heart

ii.

sometimes i am grateful just to sip air into my lungs
that slow, luxurious extravagance of inflation
the rise and fall of ribs
and tendon
and muscle
my lips reach across the darkness
groping blindly for yours,
reaching them only in my mind.
you are my most radiant light
grounded in reality
yet superseding realism
my most beautiful
        joyous
         boisterous human

iii.

i think of the imminent return to normalcy
and want to cry
look at the changing aspens
and want to cry
look at his face alight with some shared thought
and want to cry
but my heart is its own dirty traitor
and in dreams you return
looking towards me again with softness
a tickle of mischief flaring
you caress my cheek
and it could all be so easy
in a way that folds in on itself
like a paper crane

iv.

i can see myself turn to you
to share a glance across a crowded room
to find you already looking
we sear steaks in cast iron skillets
and dance around the kitchen island
(to anything but bachata)
we regale in flavour
eyes rolling back in our skulls in delight
we laugh knowingly over wine glass rims
and share cigarettes
and talk of books
and watch stupid tv
and i reach for your hand in the street
                             on the train
                             in a theatre
                                           without thinking

part of me misses every person i've cared for,
      even if they were bad to me.
part of me cries for every wrong decision i've made,
      and for every good thing they've led me to.
when the adrenaline of the day fades
and i'm left only with myself
at times i am so softhearted
i feel as though the world could break me wide open
with a single tap.

promises of reciprocal kindness
proscribed to brief spurts of ecstasy
on borrowed time   ,
           in borrowed places

am i taking the dregs given to me
to fill the void
or discrediting something beautiful
for naught but fright?

sometimes we are two minds as one
and sometimes we are childhood best friends,
riding our bikes to get ice cream
but mostly we are coworkers
yet i see the way we look at each other,
                    look to each other,
and it seems impossible to watch you walk away

so many perfect things of the future
but all of them false

he uses the dog as an excuse to inch closer
casually touching knees, both pretending that the contact
doesn't draw the breath from the room.
eyes tinged in khaki green;
clear, like an honest pond,
open in a way that terrifies me.
i catalogue this softness,
all exposed underbelly,
and i do not wish to be careless.

nothing stills my heart quite like the errant notion
of baring myself to another human.
it collects in my throat and upper spine,
drawing knots beneath my shoulder blades.
everything around me decomposes,
consumed in a slow-burning, yet unrelenting flame.
perhaps doing so for selfish reasons
is no way to give yourself to another;
quick to anger
and slow to sadness,
i do not feel better,
only tired and stiff and growing cold.

buzz of joy, buzz of gratitude
singing of the heart, even on the harshest day
cautiously,
        nervously,
i have hope raised on tiptoe
for the future

hope is a newly minted phoenix,
its crumpled body small
                      in your cupped palm.
scooped from a bed of its own cooling embers,
hope is its own rebirth
                      in the face of fire.

San Rafael, 6:39pm

he hauls himself into the car, cigarette still lit,
in urgent pursuit of the sunset lapping at our heels.
we drive up the first rise we can find,
above the houses raised into the hillside on their spindly stilts,

and i think of the intensity of childhood,
how badly i wish i had screamed like that,
cried to the heavens:

> "THIS IS FUCKED UP AND THIS IS
> A PERFECTLY VALID RESPONSE"

how many times is that so acutely felt
but rarely articulated?
how different would our lives be if we felt aloud
as fervently as we felt internally?
how much faster would we understand each other
and with how much more compassion would we respond?

it feels like a waste to mourn time lost,
or rather, time never had,
but sometimes i can't help myself from imagining
other worlds,
        other pasts;
perhaps it would make no difference at all.

i want to believe that my fascination for stories of families
stems from a desire to understand my own —
to be more patient and forgiving
of their human fallibility.
but it may also be a search to recognize my child self in another,
to witness them as i am witnessing myself.

can becoming a parent make you a better person,
if you let it?
by nature of the forced need to acknowledge
the big feelings of a little person?
i suppose that's also where many crumble,
brought to their knees by their own progeny.

the sun has set,
but the light has not yet left the sky:
cornflower blue fields,
brushed with swathes of cotton candy pink.
frogs peep their nighttime songs,
and starlings flock back to the roost.
sounds of the highway soften to the background,
like crashing waves from this high up;
streetlights come on, pinpricks in the distance,
and we too begin our journey home.

in the stranger's house
none of my desires have teeth.
but with the fizz of anticipation
sparking at the tip of my tongue,

i wish for joy in my ecstasy sandwich.

BE KIND & CARING
GIVE A LISTENING EAR

BLESS SOMEONE
TODAY

GOD LOVES YOU
JOHN 3:16-17

Kelli Fox is a multimedia interdisciplinary artist based in Telluride, CO who earned her BFA in Interrelated Media from the Massachusetts College of Art and Design. Her work exists primarily in the forms of sculptural film/video installation, poetic prose, community-driven event production, and lighting design.

Conceptually, her work focuses on curation of viewer experience, manipulation of memory over time, the paradox of guarded vulnerability, (mis-/re-/non-)connections between people, and the emotional weight of absence.

In addition to her artistic practice, Kelli is invested in studying film, reading (voraciously), cooking, carpentry, problem solving, and actively working towards operating an artist-run farm commune + residency venue.

Her writing has previously been featured in Glean Magazine and The West Review; her most recent collection will be published with Fifth Wheel Press in Fall 2022.

More of her work can be found at www.kelli-fox.work.